Lullabies
TO
Dreamland

DENIECE WILLIAMS

Illustrations by Matt Hall

HARVEST HOUSE PUBLISHERS
Eugene, Oregon 97402

This book is dedicated to Forrest, Logan, Ken, and Kevin...

and to the Lord,

who gave me something to say.

CONTENTS

GOD IS NEAR

"It's a miracle!" The words spring from our lips the moment we glimpse our baby. The wonder of a new life, precious and vulnerable, lying in our arms, awakens our hearts to our heavenly Father's presence. That is what miracles do. They remind us that God is near. There will be times as parents when we face challenges that seem overwhelming. In those times the same God who drew near to breathe the breath of life into the child we hold promises us, "I will never leave you nor forsake you."

The Lord is near to all who call upon Him.

Psalm 145:18

A Miracle Of Love

Amazingly it started with candlelight,
Suddenly everything I wore fit too tight.
The doctor said very soon there will
Be someone new,
A bundle of joy coming to you,
Smiling with eyes of brown or blue,
A miracle of love,
A miracle of love, it's true.

Your daddy and I could never
Have been prepared,
We wanted to do our best so we
Were scared.
What an awesome responsibility
To love you, guide you, your whole
Life through.
Oh what a gift God gave us in you,
A miracle of love,
A miracle of love, it's true.

I just can't explain the feeling
Right from the start,
How two became one
Reflecting what's in our hearts.

We'll love you, guide you,
Your whole life through.
Oh what a gift God gave us in you,
A miracle of love, a miracle of love,
It's true.

Words by Deniece Williams & Brad Westering

THE GIFT

"Children are a gift from God!" cries the psalmist. "Happy is the man who has his quiver
full of them." In the colorful language of another time, David presents an enduring truth.
Children are more than a miracle. They are also a blessing from the Lord. The cherished
relationship that grows between parent and child is God's gift to us. It enlarges our capacity
to love and be loved, to experience joy and pain, and to receive with simple delight
the view of life from a child's eyes.

Children are a gift from God; they are his reward.
Psalm 127:3 TLB

Baby Of Mine

I LOVE YOU SO, BABY OF MINE,
Look at those hands, your little nose,
Your eyes.
I know God knew, baby of mine,
That I'd see pieces of heaven in
Your eyes.

Only God could create you,
You're one of life's mysteries;
Oh you're so precious,
I'm glad He gave you to me;
It's easy to see you're wondrously made,
Baby of mine.

I'll hold you close, baby of mine,
Rocking you gently is simply a joy,
Baby of mine, I love you so,
I can't resist giving you kisses galore.

Only God could create you,
You're one of life's mysteries;
Oh you're so precious,
I'm glad He gave you to me;
It's easy to see you're
Wondrously made,
Baby of mine.

LEADING OUR LAMBS TO GOD

How will our little ones know Jesus loves them? They will see it in our eyes, in our touch, in our words, in our songs. They will feel the love of Jesus when we hold them, when we wipe the tears from their eyes, when we bounce them on our knees. Nothing else can match love's power. It reaches into the unseen places of the heart, and there draws a child to God.

He took them up in His arms, put His hands
on them, and blessed them.

Mark 10:16

Lamb Of God

WE'RE TOLD TO COUNT THE SHEEP
Before we go to sleep,
To watch them hop,
To watch them jump
As over the fence they leap.

Yet what's the purpose for
Without them meaning more,
I tell you now there is a One
To count on evermore.

For Jesus is the Lamb,
The Savior of all man,
So count upon Him
Knowing that He died and rose again.

In Him you will have rest
From all your weariness,
So go to sleep, my baby,
Go to sleep and rest.

For there is only One,
The Father's precious Son,
The Lamb of God who takes away
The sin of everyone.

For Jesus is the Lamb,
The Savior of all man,
So count upon Him
Knowing that He died and rose again.

Remember this is true,
He's always there for you,
So go to sleep, my baby,
Go to sleep and rest.
Jesus is the Lamb.

Words by Deniece Williams & Brad Westering

A GOOD CHOICE

As we look around, it is easy to find other parents who seem more skillful in their roles than we are. Yet God, who sees our lives from beginning to end, has chosen to unfold His love to our children uniquely through us. We bring all that we have to Jesus. He takes our offering and transforms it, like the bread and fish, into just what our little one needs. God hasn't overlooked a single thing in His plan for your child—especially you.

I have called you by name; you are Mine.

Isaiah 43:1 NASB

GOD MADE YOU SPECIAL

GOD MADE YOU SPECIAL,
God made you special,
For there's no other who's just like you,
Special you are.

For He took the time
To breathe into your heart and mind
An identity,
Your own kind of style sets you apart.
Be yourself, it's fine,
It's all God's design.

God made you special,
God made you special,
For there's no other who's just like you,
You're special, you're so special,
Special you are.

PATTERNS OF LIFE

As day follows night, so God has created seasons for our lives. In one season He gives work
to satisfy our souls. In another, He gives rest to restore our spirits. When our children
are small, the scales can seem unequally balanced. Rest may seem like a lost dream. But
when our children are grown, the time of childhood will seem like the shortest night.
Until then, the strength we need is as close as a whispered prayer.

Those who wait on the Lord shall renew their strength.
Isaiah 40:31

Brahms Lullaby

Today was such a pleasant day,
I watched you working hard at play;
You ran, you jumped, you rode your bike,
Played with your friends till suppertime.
But now it's time to say goodnight,
To shut the door and dim the lights;
Don't rub the sleep from your eyes,
I'll sing a lullaby.

Mr. Sandman, he is coming
To take baby off to dreamland,
Mr. Sandman, he is coming
To take baby off to dreamland.
While Mommy rocks you in her arms,
Mommy rocks you in her arms,
Mommy rocks you in her arms.

FRIENDS FOREVER

Abraham was called the "friend of God" because he knew and trusted God. When Jesus came to earth, He made it possible for all of us to be called by this same name. He said to His disciples, "I no longer call you servants....Instead I have called you friends" (John 15:15 NIV). Jesus' arms are open wide—to us and to our children. It is never too early to teach our little ones that Jesus is their best friend. He will help them understand who He is in a way that is perfect for them.

Let the little children come to Me, and do not forbid them.

Mark 10:14

Jesus Is Your Best Friend

When you hurt, really hurt,
Jesus' love will touch you,
Make the hurt go away,
Bring sunshine so you can play.
When you feel all alone,
You can't find a playmate,
Don't forget He's your best friend.

When you're scared, really scared,
Jesus' love protects you,
He will hear when you call,
Jesus is your all in all.
When your day's going great
Take time out to thank Him,
Don't forget He's your best friend.

Go to Jesus, go to Jesus, look to Jesus.

Friends can talk, friends can share
Every secret feeling,
Don't you hide what's inside,
You can be revealing.
Jesus is there just for you,
Take time out to know Him,
Don't forget He's your best friend.

Look to Jesus, look to Jesus, go to Jesus.

Friends can talk, friends can share
Every secret feeling.
Jesus' love will touch you,
Jesus' love protects you,
Don't forget He's your best friend.

A LITTLE CHILD SHALL LEAD THEM

Children teach us by their simplicity. They delight in the present moment; their eyes dance
with each new discovery. Unless we tarnish their trust, they start each day knowing they
are loved and cared for and close each day with confident assurance that brings sweet
dreams. Are our own dreams as sweet? Like a child who runs to a parent to kiss the hurt
away, we need to give our troubles to our Father, trusting Him to take care
of all that concerns us.

Cast all your anxiety on him because he cares for you.

1 Peter 5:7 NIV

DREAMLAND

WATCHING THE FLOWERS GROW
Playing in the snow
Splashing in the rain
Rain on the windowpane
Go to dreamland.

Wind blowing through your hair
Kites dancing in the air
Castles in the sand
A kitty in your hand
Go to dreamland.

Whatever is good and true
Dream about those things
If lovely and pure
Dream about those things
Go to dreamland.

Trees swaying in the breeze
Running through autumn leaves
Sailboats upon the sea
Go to dreamland.

PROMISES

Have you seen your children's eyes sparkle when you promise to play ball or take them on a special outing? Anticipation lights their faces with eager expectation. How much more should our faces brighten at the promises of our heavenly Father. As earthly parents, God has entrusted us with passing His promises—both for this life and the life to come—to our children. His promises are our treasure and our children's priceless inheritance.

These words...shall be in your heart; you shall teach them
diligently to your children.

Deuteronomy 6:6,7

RAINBOW

GOD SENT A RAINBOW
With colors so beautiful
Hung in the sky for you and me to see.

God sent a rainbow
Reminding Him and to let us know
All of His promises He'll keep.
He promises never to leave,
Send an angel to watch
While you sleep.
All your fears He has said
He'll relieve,
That comforts me.

God sent a rainbow,
A gift to my baby boy,
Sending peace, His love,
His joy to you.

WELCOME HOME

It takes courage to be a parent. From the moment we watch our little ones take their first steps, venturing forth on untested legs, we realize we cannot protect them from all of life's hard falls. But as they grow from childhood to adulthood, we can provide a place where their tears will be as welcome as laughter and their broken hearts can come to be mended by love. We can give our children a place where they will always find someone to stand with them—a place called home.

Love never fails.
1 Corinthians 13:8

I'll Be There

Up and down, 'round and 'round,
Sometimes fast or slowing down,
Step right up, hold on,
I'll be around.

Pretty horse on its course,
Don't be scared if you stop midair,
Take my hand, hold on,
I'll be around.

I'll be there, I'll be there,
Little children, I'll be there,
I'll be there, I'll be there,
Little children, I'll be there.

Don't you frown,
You're safe and sound,
Riding on life's merry-go-round,
Don't you sigh, hold on,
I'll be around.

Please don't cry, I'm standing by
To dry the tears from your eyes,
I won't leave you, hold on,
I'll be around.

THE ANGEL CHOIR

Angels and children seem to go together naturally. But have you ever wondered why? It's more than wishful thinking on the part of anxious parents! One day Jesus told the multitude that they must become like a child to enter the kingdom of heaven. Then He said, "Do not despise one of these little ones, for I say to you that in heaven their angels always see the face of My Father." Our children do have angels watching over them. What a comfort as we tuck our baby into bed.

He shall give His angels charge over you, to keep you in all your ways.

Psalm 91:11

Go To Sleep

TIME TO GO TO SLEEP,
So close your eyes, baby sweet,
Time to go to sleep,
So close your eyes,
Enjoy sweet sleep,

And know that the angels
Surround you
With loving care,
They're always there.
And know that the angels
Surround you
With wings open wide to cuddle
My child.

Time to say goodnight,
He'll keep you safe till morning light,
Time to say goodnight,
God's always near,
He'll hold you tight.

And know that the angels
Surround you,
They'll keep away harm
Through night, until dawn,
And know that the angels
Surround you,
They'll guard your way as you lay,
Go to sleep.

THE LOVE OF A CHILD

In a world that constantly measures people by its own standards, at least one small person loves us for just who we are. With little arms wrapped around our neck and a hug that says "I love being with you," we feel the pleasure that comes with total acceptance. A child's love is not blind, but it holds no grudges and makes no lists. Few things come as close to the Father's love for us through Jesus as the love of a child.

I have loved you with an everlasting love.

Jeremiah 31:3

Unconditional Love

UNCONDITIONAL LOVE,
That's what I get from you.
Most times you even laugh
At the things I say and do.
You run up to me
With your arms open wide
And let me take a peek
At how you feel inside.
Unconditional love,
That's what I get from you.

I can count on you
To show me the truth,
And it's easy to see
When you disapprove,
And oh the bedtime hugs you give
When the day is through.
Unconditional love,
That's what I get from you,
Unconditional love,
That's what I get from you.

GOLDEN OPPORTUNITIES

As we tuck our baby under the covers, the building blocks scattered on the floor remind us
that it has been a busy day. We've built tall towers and knocked them down again. We've
sung "Jesus Loves Me" a million times. We've made mistakes and made amends. In the
simple activities of this day, we have had the opportunity to plant in our child a spirit of
thankfulness, assurance, and forgiveness. These are spiritual building blocks
that help a child's faith grow strong.

Train a child in the way he should go, and when he is old he will not turn from it.

Proverbs 22:6 NIV

ANGEL FACE

I LOOKED INTO THE FACE
Of an angel tonight,
And in the quiet of the nursery
I remember with delight
All the little special ways
You brighten up my day;
I looked into the face of an angel tonight.

Where did you put your halo?
Did you leave it far behind
When you traveled down from heaven,
Baby of mine?
Is it in the toy chest
Or your secret hiding place?
I looked into the face of an angel tonight.

I'm not going to tell you it was a perfect day;
As hard as we both tried,
It didn't work out that way.
But as I hold you close to me
I know it's all worthwhile;
I looked into the face of an angel tonight.

GOD HEARS

The words of this familiar child's prayer remind us how dependent we are on the Lord, the giver of life. In prayer we touch the face of God, committing our lives to His daily care. Scripture illustrates the intimate nature of prayer when it pictures the prophet Samuel speaking into the ear of the Lord, and the Lord bending close to whisper back. In this same kind of private communion, we receive the assurance that God hears and answers the prayers of our parent hearts.

I love the Lord, because He has heard my voice....He has inclined His ear to me.

Psalm 116:1,2

Now I Lay Me Down To Sleep

NOW I LAY ME DOWN TO SLEEP,
I pray the Lord my soul to keep.
If I should die before I wake,
I pray the Lord my soul He'll take.

Now I lay me down to rest,
For Jesus' sake I'll do my best,
To love, to share, always be kind,
Be patient, forgiving all the time,
Amen.

THE BLESSING

Teddy bears and blankets—these tattered, familiar objects bring comfort to little ones and whisk them gently off to dreamland. By the time our children are grown, we may feel like well-worn teddy bears ourselves (slightly frayed around the edges, but dearer for the use). We will release our precious offspring into the world, having taught them to dream the dreams of God. By God's grace, our children will be able to say:

The lines have fallen to me in pleasant places; indeed,
my heritage is beautiful to me.

Psalm 16:6 NASB

MR. SLEEPY EYE

YOUR FAVORITE LITTLE BUDDY
Is laying in your bed.
He's been waiting for you,
You little sleepy head.

It's Mr. Sleepy Eye,
A special nighttime friend.
You cuddled him this morning
When your day began.

Now he'll take you off to dreamland
While Mommy's softly singing
For you my little baby
A sweet lullaby.

Who sees you in the morning,
Who sees you every night,
Who wears a night cap on his head
And has a funny smile.

When the stars have filled the sky,
Who helps your dreams take flight,
Who's cuddly soft,
It's Mr. Sleepy Eye.

Now he'll take you off to dreamland
While Mommy's softly singing
For you my little baby
A sweet lullaby.

The first eleven lyrics in this book are taken from the album by the same name, produced by Word, Inc. and are used by permission of the author in conjunction with Word, Inc.

LULLABIES TO DREAMLAND
Copyright © 1993 by Eleine, Inc.
Published by Harvest House Publishers
Eugene, Oregon 97402

Williams, Deniece.
  Lullabies to dreamland / Deniece Williams.
    p. cm.
  Summary: A collection of poems that provide bedtime reassurances of love, including God's love.
    ISBN 1-56507-149-2
    1. Children's poetry.   2. Lullabies.   3. Bedtime--Poetry.
4. Sleep--Poetry. [1. Lullabies. 2. Bedtime--Poetry.
3. Christian life--Poetry. 4. American poetry--Afro-American authors.]
    I. Title.
PN6109.97.W55 1993
398.8--dc20

                                                93-804
                                                 CIP
                                                 AC